Ellen Peterson

D0936349

SPORTS ILLUSTRATED
BOOK OF SKIING

SPORTS ILLUSTRATED

Book of

SKIING

BY THE EDITORS OF
SPORTS ILLUSTRATED

J. B. LIPPINCOTT COMPANY
Philadelphia and New York

COPYRIGHT © 1957, BY TIME INC.
PRINTED IN THE UNITED STATES OF AMERICA
LIBRARY OF CONGRESS CATALOG CARD NUMBER: 60-7841

SECOND IMPRESSION

CONTENTS

Text by Willy Schaeffler and Ezra Bowen
Art by Robert Riger

SPORTS ILLUSTRATED
BOOK OF SKIING

Willy Schaeffler, Director of Ski Events for the 1960 Winter Olympics, demonstrates a stop turn on a steep slope, utilizing the reverse shoulder method of the shortswing technique.

THE FIRST LESSON: PRESEASON EXERCISES

To anyone used to skiing with the Arlberg or French technique, the most startling new movements in the short-swing are the reverse shoulder, the heel thrust and the comma position. In the old techniques, shoulder rotation was the key to all direction changes, and the shoulder swing was a powerful movement that pulled your skis around through the snow. For example, in a turn to the left, the skier began by winding his shoulders back to the right like a sidearm pitcher getting ready to throw. Then he swung his shoulders around to the left, and the force of this rotation swung the skis to the left, with the tips pointing the new direction and the backs of the skis following along like the rear wheels of an automobile. The important thing was to keep a firm connection between the upper and lower body so that the skis responded instantly to any shoulder movement. These rotation turns were abetted by much up-and-down movement in the knees and hips to take weight off the backs of the skis. And as the skier swung through the turn, he leaned inward like a bicycle rider going around a corner. There was no emphasis on heel thrust because the shoulder swing was so powerful that any

1

added heel thrust was likely to make the skier turn too far, leaving the skis pointed back up the hill with the skier starting a slow, reluctant schuss backward down the slope.

In the shortswing, however, everything is different. Shoulder rotation is out, and turns are made with an easy, natural rhythm. In every turn, the shoulders lag behind, following *after* the skis have been set in the new direction. The new turning force is a subtle outward thrust of the heels, not a violent push; and as he thrusts with his heels the skier actually twists his shoulders back in the opposite direction from the turn. Instead of bending forward from the hips, the skier keeps his upper body almost erect. And instead of leaning in toward the center of the turn, he leans his upper body out over the skis, with his knees and

Shortswing turn, shown in swing by Schaeffler, cuts out tiring rotation and up-and-down-weighting of traditional Arlberg and French techniques. Entire force for new turn shown here comes from thrust by legs and heels, with hips and upper body bent into comma-like position (*right*) at climax of turn as counterforce for leg thrust. Shoulders, instead of leading turn, swivel in opposite direction, squaring around only when skier is ready to start new turn.

hips curved toward slope in the comma position.

Now, all this is pretty powerful stuff for any beginner, and perhaps even puzzling to the expert schooled in the old rotation technique. To make it simpler, Schaeffler has worked out the living room exercises shown on the following pages as a dryland cram course in the new technique. By practicing these exercises you can, without even putting on a ski, get the feeling of the basic movements in the shortswing turn and get some idea why your shoulders have to be swiveled around in the reverse position and your body bent into the comma. Better still, while you work on these exercises you will at the same time be conditioning the muscles that you will use when you actually begin to ski.

3

The Schaeffler exercises are geared directly to the shortswing. The ones on pages 4-11 are quite easy to do. If you are in good condition, you can ignore the beginners' limits given for each exercise and just keep doing them until you get tired. The ones on the succeeding pages, however, take a little straining, and if you suspect that you are the least bit out of shape leave them alone for a week until your skiing muscles tone up. When you do start them, begin with the number of repetitions that Willy recommends and don't increase the dose too fast.

Shortswing jump reproduces motions of new turning technique. Stand with feet together, then jump quickly from side to side. Note how heels thrust out as toes touch floor, shoulders lag behind hips, and body assumes comma position at end of each jump. Twenty times.

Having worked on your exercises for three weeks, you will be able to move right into the shortswing classes with some confidence in your ability to make the movements in the new turn. Thus you can be sure of a full day of good skiing the first time out instead of having to waste half your time resting at the bottom of the slope.

Change-step jump starts with right foot in front of left, right shoulder advanced, body bent left in comma. Exerciser jumps up, switches position of feet and reverses shoulders before landing. This prepares skier for maneuvers in which legs swing in opposite direction from upper body, also conditions legs, chest muscles. Ten times right and left.

Heel thrust shows real source of turning power in shortswing. Stand with feet together, knees slightly flexed. In one quick motion, squat down no more than six inches and thrust heels to left or right. Let the shoulders lag, then square them off and straighten up and you will find you have turned about 45°. Since balance is tricky in this exercise, beginners should stand next to wall or chair. Fifteen times.

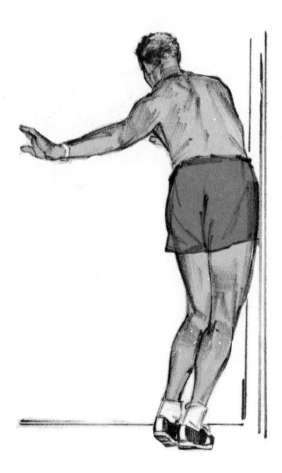

Ankle touch shows why downhill shoulder must be held back to allow skier to keep flexible comma position. Standing with knees slightly flexed, shoulders squared, try to touch right ankle with right hand. It's almost impossible. Now pull back right shoulder, and body easily bends so that hand can reach ankle. Ten times right and left.

Comma bend strengthens and stretches body muscles used in basic traverse position as well as in long traverse when skier propels himself by thrusting with the downhill ski, as shown at left. Start with feet spread, arms over head. Shift weight to left leg and slowly bend left knee with right knee straight, at same time bending upper body to right. Hold for count of three. Five times, right and left.

Stork stretch is one-legged balancing exercise that reflects comma position, prepares skier for turns and traverses in which weight will be concentrated on downhill ski. For this exercise, stand with feet together, left hand over head, and slowly bend to right until left leg is parallel with floor. Hold position for a count of five. Three times each side.

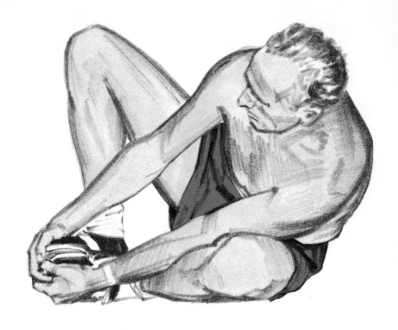

Buddha squat toughens stomach muscles for body control in rough terrain, also stretches thigh, hip muscles to give them looseness needed in shortswing's rhythmic turns. Begin exercise by sitting on floor with soles of feet together, knees spread out to sides, hands gripping toes to hold them together. Slowly roll over onto one leg, and keep rolling down onto your shoulder until you are lying on your back. Then roll back up the same way you came down. If you don't make it, keep fighting awhile. The first week you probably won't be able to roll back. When you make it, you are ready to try the exercise twice. Until then, once is plenty.

Rock and roll stretches virtually all muscles in front part of body, arms and legs. Lie down on stomach, bend knees until you can reach back and grab each instep with hand. Once you have hold of your feet, pull with arms, arch back and raise head. Rock forward and back three times, rest for a moment, then rock three more times.

Phantom chair is toughener for thigh muscles, which act as shock absorbers on bumpy runs, give initial force to heel thrust in turns. Stand with back to wall, feet 18 inches out from base of wall. Sink down to a sitting position, hold for 15 seconds, then rest and try again. When you get so you can count to 30, try it on one leg.

15

Jackknife jump strengthens thighs, stomach, Achilles' tendons, helps coordination and timing vital to rhythmic shortswing. Stand erect, jump up and touch toes with knees as straight as possible, land on the toes. Five times.

Stooper's strut stretches the Achilles' tendons, back muscles, also helps with balance. Bend and grasp toes; keep the knees straight, then start walking. Women, more supple in lower body than men, take 20 steps, men take 10.

Slow roll is falling exercise, teaches skier to relax in unfamiliar position, also strengthens stomach, leg muscles. Skier in correct comma position tends to fall out over slope—scarier but safer than falling into slope—and then rolls backward. To condition body for such falls, lie on back, arms out, and raise legs, with knees stiff, until toes touch floor behind head. Do slow side split, return to original position. Three times.

Airplane spin loosens arms and upper body, strengthens thighs, helps timing and also teaches skier to relax when feet are off ground and body is turning in air. Spread feet, crank shoulders back, then jump and unwind, making complete turn in air. If full turn makes you dizzy, start with half turns. Three times each way.

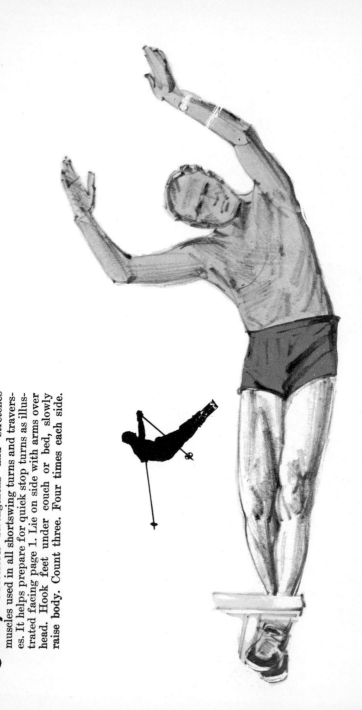

Lazy comma strengthens and stretches muscles used in all shortswing turns and traverses. It helps prepare for quick stop turns as illustrated facing page 1. Lie on side with arms over head. Hook feet under couch or bed, slowly raise body. Count three. Four times each side.

20

Split jump strengthens leg and arm muscles, also conditions small muscles in feet and ankle which take so much of the strain in comma position and heel-thrust turns. Stand straight with feet together, jump up and do fore-and-aft split. Land on toes and jump again, switching leg and arm positions in air. Ten times.

Dry skating imitates position used in leg-pushing traverse and in normal skating. From standing start, leap forward, spreading arms. Land on toes, then jump to other foot. Twelve times.

21

Front split loosens thighs and hips,
stretches and strengthens groin muscles
used in heel-brushing snow plow of shortswing technique. Begin exercise by lying
on stomach. Do push-up and hold arms
stiff. Then throw feet forward and out so
that feet land on same line on floor as
hands. Jump back to prone position. Five
times.

2

TRAVERSES AND BASIC TURNS

In the preceding section, Willy Schaeffler demonstrated 17 living room exercises to prepare you for the supple heel thrust and reverse shoulder turns in this new method. Now he shows under actual skiing conditions how the shortswing really works.

To assist with the demonstrations, Willy drafted Mrs. Vernon (Ann) Taylor, wife of one of Denver's leading businessmen. Ann was an accomplished skier in the shoulder-rotating Arlberg technique. But after one day with Willy she was converted to the new method. On the second day, she mastered the basic movements up through the stem turn. Any advanced intermediate can catch on as quickly as Ann. Beginners will probably take longer, but by using the teaching aids that Willy and Ann show on the following pages, they will be able to learn more easily and with more pleasure than with any other system of skiing.

New downhill position is upright, with only slight flexing of knees, ankles; no hip bend, hands above waist. Poles are four inches longer to help keep skier erect, should reach within hand's breadth of armpit.

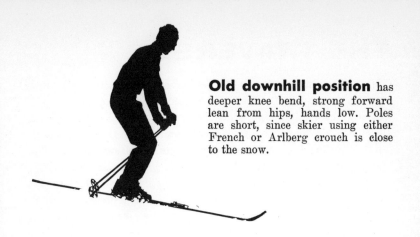

Old downhill position has deeper knee bend, strong forward lean from hips, hands low. Poles are short, since skier using either French or Arlberg crouch is close to the snow.

THE TRAVERSE

In the shortswing, the basic maneuver, from which all other moves develop, is the traverse, in which the skier moves diagonally across the slope. And the basic position is the striking new comma, shown below. In the comma, the downhill shoulder is pulled back and the weight is on the downhill ski. The upper body is over the skis, with the hips, knees and ankles curved toward the slope. This idea of beginning with the traverse is a direct departure from the Arlberg method, which starts from the snowplow. It differs, too, from the French method, which builds from a traverse but keeps the shoulders squared and demands a powerful forward lean at the knees and hips. In the comma, by contrast, the upper body is loose, relaxed, ready to move with subtle, rhythmic motions rather than powerful swings.

Perfect comma on a flat surface shows knees, ankles together so skis form single unit. On slope, skier should look ahead, advance upper skis two to four inches.

Learning comma, Ann gets her down-hill shoulder back, but keeps hips, knees locked in incorrect straight-on position. Willy has body curved in correct comma. Heavy lines dramatize difference between shortswing and other traverse techniques.

Ankle touch while moving in traverse helps skier to keep shoulder back, body flexible. As exercise shows in Section 1, skier with squared shoulders is able to reach only to knee.

Lifting uphill ski forces weight onto the down-hill ski, upper body leaning out over slope. Natural reaction on steep hill is to lean toward slope, danger-ous in fall since shoulders will hit while skis are still planted in snow, causing a bad twist.

SIDE-SLIPPING

The next step in the shortswing is the side-slip, a practical way for any novice to come down a hill and a good way for anyone to practice the all-important business of edge control, *i.e.*, the angle at which your skis bite into the slope during a traverse. Like every shortswing maneuver, it begins and ends with the comma, with a minimum of motion in between. For the side-slip, in fact, there is no new movement beyond an unweighting of the skis through a downward motion, and a releasing of the uphill edges that allows you to go into a controlled slide.

Side-slip begins with Willy in traverse position **(1).** To start side-slip he unweights skis by bending knees and hips down and farther toward slope in exaggeration of comma, at same time easing grip of uphill edges on snow by slight outward turn of the ankles **(2).** By accentuating comma bend, Willy keeps upper body out over skis, thus correcting natural tendency to lean into slope when edges let go, upsetting balance and causing skis to chatter or slide out from under you. To stop side-slip, Willy downweights again, then returns to modified comma, rolling edges back **(3)** until skis take hold. If skis will not slide easily, try exercises shown on pp. 32, 36, and 37.

Two-pole push is a good way for beginner to learn side-slip. Stand in comma position on side of hill, hold poles together as shown, and push against the slope. As you bend knees and hips to put pressure on poles, skis become unweighted and you start to side-slip. Poles act as brace to prevent fall into slope when skis first begin to slide.

Half side-slip, graduate version of straight side-slip, is excellent exercise in edge control, besides being quick, easy way to make diagonal descent. Skier, moving in fast traverse, releases edges as shown in figures on pp. 30 and 31. As edges let go, forward motion makes skis carve diagonal path through snow with upper edges brushing snow as in advanced turns to come.

Parallel poles placed across front of torso show how hips, shoulders must be kept in same plane during side-slip and traverse. Skiers trying shortswing for first time often move downhill shoulder forward, twisting body off balance, breaking comma and forcing upper body in toward the slope.

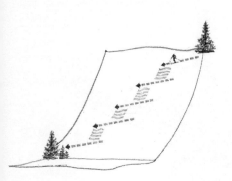

Patterns on snow show paths of skis during straight side-slip (*left*) and half side-slip. In straight side-slip, Willy moves slowly, stops, side-slips, moves on. In half side-slip he skims across slope in one continuous move, stopping only when he has reached bottom.

Push and catch is good confidence builder for side-slip since skis cannot run away. Plant one pole just above uphill ski, other pole downhill. Push with uphill pole. Skis will slide; stop at downhill pole.

Split push is good side-slip aid in heavy snow or in steep narrow gullies where the skier has no room to maneuver. Plant both poles uphill, one at each end of skis, release edges and push to start side-slip.

THE FIRST TURN

There are only two ways a skier can turn—in toward the slope
or out toward the fall line, the line of steepest descent down
a hill. Your first shortswing turn (*above and right*) is toward
the slope—a nice, safe way to go, and one that takes very
little effort. Starting in a traverse, and using the edge control
and unweighting by downward movement learned in side-
slipping, you add one small ingredient: a gentle outward
thrust of the heels that sets the skis swinging in an arc across
the snow. Starting a turn by heel push is one of the great
shortswing innovations, in contrast to the Arlberg and French
techniques, where the turn impulse is a shoulder swing trans-
mitted to the fronts of the skis.

Rear view of swing to slope shows Willy moving in slow traverse (1) on easy beginner's hill. To start turn impulse he pulls downhill shoulder a bit farther to the rear to prepare for heel thrust. As in side-slip, he unweights skis by bending knees and hips down and more toward slope. With shoulders back and comma increased (2), skis have already started to turn. Then, with outward and downward thrust of heels (3), Willy swings skis through 45° arc. Again imitating side-slip, he stops turn by edging skis (4), then easing comma to start off in a new traverse.

Front view of swing to slope, done on steeper hill than rear view, as seen in illustration on pp. 38-39, gives clear look at difference between easy comma in traverse and strong comma at point of heel thrust in turn. On gentle slope, Schaeffler needed old-fashioned forward bend from the hip to get momentum for last part of turn. On steep hill, natural speed from the terrain provides all necessary forward push. Willy's position at end of swing, and all his movements through this turn, are identical to those of advanced turns to come.

40

Learning swing, Ann shows hangover from old technique in bringing downhill shoulder forward. As teaching aid, Willy crooks poles inside elbows, which helps force downhill shoulder back. Ann tries it (*below*) and finds it works—shoulder back, she now can start her swing in the correct position.

Treetop view of shortswing into slope shows downhill shoulder and hip drawn well back, body bent in comma, knees, ankles flexed to start heel thrust.

Turning over bump, (*right*) Ann uses natural fallaway of terrain to unweight backs of skis for heel push and swing. Learning to read terrain, using natural hill contours to help turns, makes skiing much easier. Note Anns excellent comma, shoulder pulled back in a strong reverse position.

THE SNOWPLOW

Once you get the feeling of edge control, you are ready for
the snowplow, the best maneuver for controlling your speed
in your first turn through the fall line. This is the most despised
of all maneuvers—many experts sneer at it as a beginner's
crutch, and beginners hate it because they are usually prodded
into it before they have learned to use their edges, with the
results shown by Ann (*right*). With edge control, however,
there is nothing for the novice to worry about. Just relax and
brush out with the tails of the skis. As for the skeptical experts,
Schaeffler points out that Toni Sailer used the snowplow as a
brake in winning the Olympic downhill. Furthermore, the heel-
brushing snowplow that Willy demonstrates is a shortcut to
the linked parallel turns he will teach in Section 3.

Common mistake of experienced skiers
is to bend knees too far, spread backs of skis too
wide. Skis must be brushed gently, not forced.

Worst mistake by beginners is to try snowplow before learning edge control. If outside edges dig in, result is stiff jackknife position (*top*). If unequal pressure is put on inside edges (*bottom*), skis will start to cross.

Perfect snowplow starts (*left*) with Willy in downhill position, hands at height of belt, knees flexed, body upright but relaxed. To go into plow, Willy pushes heels out, making tails of skis slither across snow into plow position (*center*). At same time he bends knees slightly to unweight tails of skis and put slight pressure on inside edges. Note that knees are barely more than a hand's breadth apart, not spread wide with subsequent strain on thighs. Once in good plow Willy eases heel push, puts slight weight accent on inside edges (3) in order to start the skis running back together into the normal downhill position. As an edge-control exercise, try brushing in and out of snowplow 3 to 5 times in 20 yards.

Using terrain to help learn the snowplow turn, beginners swing through wide gully, using lift from counterslope at side of gully to un-weight upper ski, help start turn.

Snowplow turn, first full turn through fall line, combines snowplow (*above and right*) with comma, edge control learned in side-slip, and swing to slope. Willy starts off traversing slope in snowplow position **(1).** To turn, he pulls uphill shoulder back, shifts weight by leaning out over uphill ski **(2).** As soon as weight shift starts, skis begin to turn. Halfway through turn **(3),** Willy is heading straight down fall line, speed controlled by plow with slight pressure on inside edges, left side of body in comma, left ski carving arc of turn. Once past fall line, Willy eases comma **(4),** moves downhill shoulder forward, finishes sequence in normal snowplow position **(5)** ready to start new traverse and turn.

49

THE STEM TURN

This is the climax of your basic instruction in the shortswing. On the preceding pages you were taught the comma, the side-slip and the snowplow. These necessary fundamentals must be learned well, for in them are all the elements of the more advanced stem turn shown at right. A stem, as demonstrated (*right*) is half a snowplow. That is, you brush outward with the tail of one ski instead of two, leaving the other leg and ski still pointed in the original direction. Now, there are only two ways to stem—uphill and downhill. Willy shows both (*right*) as he prepares to make a turn to the left. In the right-hand figure Willy does it the old way, stemming with the downhill ski, weight on the uphill ski, uphill shoulder twisted back in the windup ready to start the powerful rotation that will set him into the turn. Obviously there is some waste motion here. Willy wants to turn downhill, but according to the old doctrine he must start by counterrotating and stemming away from the direction of the turn. In the left-hand figure he shows the economy of movement that is the essence of the new shortswing. He wants to turn to the left, so he takes his uphill ski and stems in the direction he wants to go. The right shoulder is back, not as a windup for rotation, but to facilitate the weight shift onto the right ski. Thus, with little more than a shifting of weight, the shortswing stem brings the skier down any slope, under any snow conditions, with more style and rhythm and far less fatigue than ever before.

50

New and old methods for starting stem turn point up dramatic departure of shortswing from old techniques. Willy starts shortswing turn (*left*) by stemming uphill ski and shifting weight, old-style turn by downhill stem and counterrotation. Note deep bend of uphill knee in old system puts heavy strain on skier's thigh.

Starting stem turn, Willy traverses gentle slope in comma position (1), downhill shoulder back, weight on downhill ski. Without shifting weight, he stems uphill ski (2) in direction of turn, pulls uphill shoulder back to prepare for weight shift. Next instant he transfers weight to uphill ski (3), and turn begins. As he comes through fall line

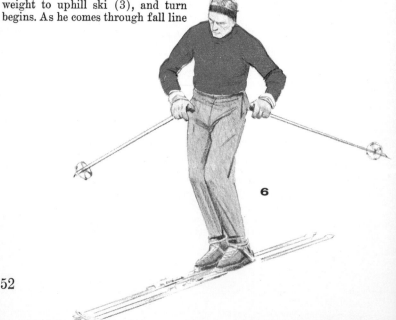

(4), weight is on outside ski, left side of body shows comma as in snowplow, but with inside ski angled more toward fall line. Once past fall line, Willy eases comma (5), lets skis run together naturally, starts new traverse (6). Stem turn, like snowplow turn, should be used only when turning out toward the fall line, not for turn into the slope.

53

Finishing stem turn, Willy and Ann
show perfect comma position as they complete
a turn to the left. Knees, ankles are flexed,
weight is on downhill ski, uphill ski unweighted,
ready to stem for turn to the right.

SWING TURNS
AND WEDELN

Holding snowplow
during stem toward fall line
on steep hill helps skier control speed in stem-turn-swing.

The graceful turns shown in this final chapter on the Austrian shortswing as taught by Willy Schaeffler are the culmination of all the lessons learned in Parts One and Two. They are the most useful, most exciting ski maneuvers ever devised. Yet they are no harder to learn than the simple stem and snowplow shown earlier. Now, Willy shows how to combine a series of swing turns in a climactic presentation of the hip-waggling ski dance called *Wedeln* (pronounced *Vay*deln), which through the past few years has been the most thoroughly discussed and most thoroughly misunderstood word in skiing's colorful lexicon.

55

Stem-turn-swing is transition step between stem turn demonstrated earlier and swing turns shown on following pages. In basic stem turn, skier starts by stemming the uphill ski until it points into the arc of the turn. He holds stem through fall line, then lets skis run back naturally into new traverse position. In swing turn, all or part of turn is carried out by parallel heel brush done with skis pressed together. Stem-turn-swing, as name implies, begins with stem, ends with swing. Basically, it is an exercise, but it is also useful way to swing past obstacles during traverse. Willy starts off in traverse **(1)**, stems toward fall line **(2)** with uphill (in this case, the right) ski. Note, however, that he does not pull back his uphill shoulder since he does not hold stem through the fall line. Moving faster as he approaches the fall line, Willy shifts weight back to downhill ski, brings skis together **(3)**, bends into comma with strong reverse shoulder. Then he thrusts out and down with heels, exaggerating knee bend to emphasize thrust **(4)** and sends tails of skis brushing across snow in swing away from the fall line, finishes by easing comma **(5)** for new traverse.

Snow pattern shows Willy does not cross fall line. Making series of stem-turn-swings gives skier feel of the rhythmic motion of linked heel-thrust turns.

Willy shows pupil how to stem into fall line, then swing back toward slope without using shoulder rotation. Moving along in slow traverse, Willy stems out lightly, then snaps skis back together and brushes with both heels.

THE STEM SWING

The stem swing is the last step before the pure parallel swing; but it is far more than just a learning device. It is a stylish and functional turn, good on any slope and good enough for anyone but the real expert. If, on the other hand, you are already an expert, you may want to start your whole shortswing curriculum with the stem swing. Be warned—hardly anyone who skis with the old style really believes he can get through the fall line with no rotation until he has tried it with a few slow, simple snowplow turns. And until a skier believes he can make it without rotation, he is likely to keep rotating—a great waste of time and effort. However, if you are in a hurry and feel you are good enough to skip some fundamental moves, let the stem swing be your first turn through the fall line. But don't make it without practicing the side-slip, the swing to the slope and a solid dose of the stem-turn-swing.

Starting stem swing (*left*), Willy traverses slope in comma position **(1)**, stems out **(2)** with uphill ski (*right ski here*) and pulls back uphill shoulder just as in stem turn. At same time he shifts weight onto uphill ski to start skis moving into arc of turn. At this point, similarity to stem turn ends. Instead of holding stem through fall line and letting skis run together slowly after turn has been completed, Willy starts bringing inside, or left, ski over to right ski even before he reaches fall line. By time Willy hits fall line **(3)** skis are almost parallel, weight completely on outer ski with inner ski barely brushing snow. Right side of body describes modified comma. Just over fall line, Willy brings skis completely parallel, bends ankles, knees and hips into strong comma **(4)**, finishes turn with outward and downward thrust by both heels, then eases comma bend **(5)** for new traverse or turn.

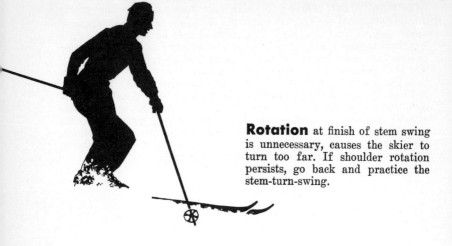

Rotation at finish of stem swing is unnecessary, causes the skier to turn too far. If shoulder rotation persists, go back and practice the stem-turn-swing.

Antirotation exercise, with poles behind neck, trains skier to keep downhill shoulder back during swing to slope.

Steep slope, (*above*) or long convex ridge is best place to practice the stem swing. Stem while moving in slow traverse, then swing into fall line. Speed from slope helps heel thrust, steep drop-off unweights tails of skis.

Lifting uphill ski during follow-through to stem swing through the fall line keeps skier from leaning in toward the slope, also checks rotation since shoulder swing will throw the skier off balance when uphill ski is raised.

THE PARALLEL
SHORTSWING

Up till now the main force for starting every turn through the
fall line has been a stemming of the uphill ski. But now the stem
disappears. The entire turn is done with the skis parallel. This
means two things. First, it means that a new turning impetus
is needed to replace the stem. That impetus is a slight forward
and upward movement made by the knees and ankles with the
help of the inside pole. The pole also provides a kind of pivot for
the turn and gives the skier learning the maneuver for the first
time something extra to push against during his heel thrust.
Willy and Ann show the difference between a parallel swing and
a stem turn at the key moment of a turn to the left. Willy demonstrates it with an exaggerated pole push just after he crosses the
fall line, Ann with an exaggerated uphill stem just before she
comes into the fall line. The disappearance of the stem has one
other meaning: Willy's instruction throughout the rest of this
final lesson is on the expert level for those who can enjoy a sport
only when they can do it as well as can possibly be done.

Using pole (*above left*) to replace stem (*right*) as basic turning force, Willy exaggerates comma to demonstrate swiveling action of hips, pushes on pole to aid heel brush. Skiers learning to use pole should minimize knee action, forward and upward movement of the body, keep pole use light and fluid.

Parallel swing through fall line begins with Willy traversing in comma position **(1)**. To start turning action he inserts downhill pole (*right pole here*) about three feet ahead of boots with easy forward roll of right shoulder, forearm and wrist **(2)**. As right shoulder comes forward, left shoulder automatically starts to fall back into reverse position. Note that pole arm stays bent, elbow fairly close to body. Weight stays directly over skis as Willy prepares for outward push of heels that sends skis swinging into arc of turn. When pole sets firmly in snow, natural lift from hand and arm pressure on pole plus light forward-and-up motion with knees and ankles brings Willy almost erect **(3)**. This subtle upward movement of body unweights tails of skis to facilitate heel thrust. As Willy comes into fall line, left side of upper body begins to assume comma again. Right ski, which will now be uphill ski, starts to move ahead, but knees and ankles are still pressed together. Just over fall line **(4)**, Willy shifts weight onto downhill ski (*now the left ski*), bends into strong comma for heel-brushing followthrough. Hips act as swivel while downhill shoulder comes back to provide counterforce for heel push. At end of turn **(5)**, Willy's downhill shoulder is still well back, tails of skis still brushing over snow. Skiing at slow speeds or in heavy snow, skier needs slightly more lift to start turn.

5

67

Too much lean forward at end of turn weights upper ski, destroys balance.

Separating skis breaks turntable of locked ankles, makes ragged turn.

Getting into swing of parallel turn, Willy practices by making series of scalloped swings. With first swing he makes simple turn to slope, needs no help from the pole to start heel push. The next three swings come closer to fall line, require help from pole. With pole use perfected, Willy returns to top of the hill (*lower right*) to make turn through fall line over entire length of slope. As exercise, keep making swings to slope, heading closer to fall line with each swing.

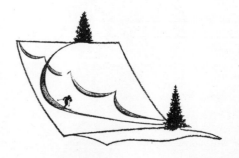

68

HOP TO THE WEDELN

Before Willy shows how to do the *Wedeln,* some of the confusion surrounding this word should be cleared up for the benefit of the thousands of skiers who have been puzzling over it for the past couple of years. To begin with, *Wedeln* is a common German word meaning "tail-wagging." In skiing it is used to describe the hip-swinging action that takes place when a skier links a fast series of parallel shortswing turns. It is not a separate technique, but merely a term for this climactic phase of the shortswing. In any case, it should not be confused with a tricky and basically undefinable maneuver called the mambo, a loose term that can be applied to any one of the dozens of personal interpretations of reverse-shoulder skiing.

Regardless of definition, there is no greater thrill in skiing than to dance down a fresh slope, carving your own track with a rhythmic series of shortswing turns. There are two ways to learn to make this kind of track—and call it *Wedeln* if you want. One way is to go from a slow schuss into a series of hopping turns. The other is by linking a tighter and tighter sequence of stem swings, blending in light thrusts with alternate poles until the lift from the pole provides the starting force for the turn and the stem disappears. The hop is the more difficult of the two and requires a bit more coordination. Willy finds that high school and college-age skiers take to it most readily. However, any accomplished skier is invited to try, and if you can do it, you can learn the *Wedeln* more quickly this way.

Best route from top of hill to bottom is winding track made by series of shortswing turns. Linking turns, as shown above, skier can—by varying length of traverses and arc of turns—control speed, swing past obstacles, pick best terrain for each maneuver.

Best exercise to prepare for hop to *Wedeln* is shortswing jump shown earlier. Note how position of Schaeffler's knees, hips and shoulders in living room exercise reflect the movements of shortswing sequence on pp. 72-73.

Mambo is any kind of individualistic variation on reverse-shoulder skiing. Execution depends on whim of performer, and since mambo lacks definite form skier can easily fall into exaggeration of reverse shoulder that leads to awkward arm position and tiring leg action shown above. Note strong forward lean in knees and ankles, sweeping arm swing that adds delayed shoulder rotation to heel thrust and reverse shoulder of the standard shortswing technique.

Quick way to learn *Wedeln* is to pick a long, even slope with about a 15° pitch. Start down fall line in slow schuss **(1),** then begin lifting tails of skis together **(2)** about six inches off snow by quick upward flicks of heels and knees. Keep hopping along until you get an even rhythm to your heel kicks; then start using poles alternately with each hop, left-right, left-right **(3).** Keep same relaxed wrist and forearm action as in pure parallel turn. When poles blend smoothly with hopping action, start thrusting with heels from one side to the other as you hop **(4),** gradually reducing upward hop and increasing side thrust until hop is gone and skis are slithering over snow in series of graceful linked turns. Tracks (*page 73*) show ski and shoulder positions at each stage of the hop to the *Wedeln.*

3

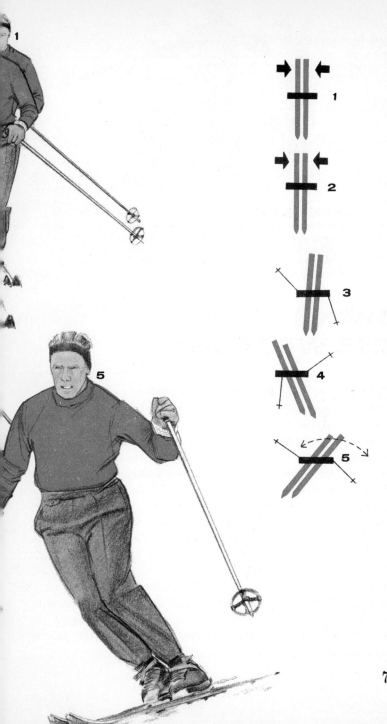

73

Swinging pendulum is impression given by good shortswing skier linking turns on fast run. Head remains almost on the same plane, shoulders and upper body barely move. The legs, ankles and heels carry out turning action,. hips act as a swivel while skis swing from side to side.

SWING TO
THE WEDELN

If you suspect that you may not be as athletic as you once were or, to be more dignified about it, if you are more interested in smooth style than in fast learning, try stem-swinging your way to the *Wedeln*. As noted, the hop is a fine shortcut for youngsters who are in a hurry to learn the ultimate in the shortswing technique and have the coordination to do a little fancy jumping around. But the hop is definitely an athletic road to *Wedeln*. There is bound to be a slight thump as the tails of the skis drop back onto the snow, and it calls for strong muscles and perfect leg control to prevent a kind of jerkiness at the end of each turn. This may be all right in a slalom gate but is unnecessarily rough and tiring for the average recreational skier. The stem-swing method, on the other hand, starts off with no lifting action whatever, just a smooth brushing back and forth over the snow as you stem first one ski, then the other, gradually bringing the skis parallel and using only the gentlest lift from the pole as the stem disappears altogether.

Swing without poles is simple parallel swing to slope from traverse, helps remind pupil that main turning action is entirely below the waist, is also good exercise for skiers who tend to overemphasize pole use by reaching too far, with resultant loss of balance.

Sure way to learn *Wedeln* is to combine series of linked stem-swing turns similar to the one taught earlier. As with the hop to the *Wedeln*, start off in a schuss—almost any reasonable slope will do, since balance is surer with the stemswing than with the hop. When you are underway in your schuss, stem out with one ski—here the right ski **(1)**. Then bring other ski parallel to it, thrust gently with both heels and immediately stem out with the opposite ski **(2)**. Keep stemming and thrusting in shorter- and shorter-radius turns until you begin to feel the rhythmic pendulum effect shown here. When your rhythm is well established, start reducing the angle of your stem **(3)** and begin blending the poles into each turn. Then, as the poles become a natural part of the turning action, eliminate the stem altogether **(4)**, making each turn with the pole and heel-brush alone, skis parallel. This is the *Wedeln*. Now, to see Willy run through a perfect *Wedeln* from start to finish, turn the page.

4

2

3

Dipsy-doodle, trick maneuver popularized years
ago by U.S. Olympian Dick Durrance, becomes valu-
able *Wedeln* exercise in shortswing. Start downhill in
snowplow, then thrust with first one heel, then the
other, with upper body loose. Hip and knee action
imitates *Wedeln*.

PERFECT WEDELN

The dramatic turning sequence shown below is the climax of Willy Schaeffler's presentation of the Austrian shortswing. This is the ultimate in parallel skiing, and there is virtually no slope or type of snow for which this technique is not ideally suited. In deep powder or crust, the skis slither through the soft lower layers of snow rather than coming out and breaking through unevenly. In wet snow the lack of shoulder swing eliminates the need for a powerful follow-through. And on a packed slope with a light dusting of powder, there is nothing, absolutely nothing, to compare with the *Wedeln*.

Top view of Willy doing *Wedeln* shows that shoulders remain almost perpendicular to fall line during turn, while elbow stays bent and relaxed as Willy swings arm forward to insert pole. Weight is on downhill (*i.e.*, left) ski, with uphill ski advanced.

Start of Wedeln—swing to left is actually finish of previous swing to right. Note in figure **1** how Willy's body is in comma, skis kicking up snow at finish of heel thrust from previous turn. At same instant, however, he brings left hand forward to plant pole, stops heel brush **(2)** as pole makes contact with snow to provide slight lift **(3)** that unweights tails of skis for the next thrust with heels.

Continuing Wedeln sequence, with tails of skis still unweighted from lift by pole, Willy begins new heel thrust **(4)** as body starts to bend into comma to provide counterforce for thrust. As aid for learning *Wedeln,* give slight outward push with pole just before it pulls free of snow. Comma increases **(5)** as Willy swings farther into turn, weight on downhill ski (the right ski in this case), upper ski ahead, knees and ankles pressed together, with skis making single track. Right hand has already started forward to place pole for next maneuver. Finish of turn **(6)** comes with final thrust of heels, right pole already in snow for the next turn, eyes fixed on the terrain ahead.

REVIEW:
THE COMPLETE
SHORTSWING

Basic position in shortswing is comma, in which weight is on the downhill ski, knees and ankles pressed together and bent toward slope. Hips are also bent toward slope, but upper body leans out from slope to maintain balance. This is traverse position from which short-swing maneuvers start. For example, by increasing knee bend and relaxing edges, skier can side-slip. By starting in traverse, then thrusting out with heels, he can swing toward slope.

Major transition from parallel swing to slope is snowplow, used for controlling speed in fall line. Once skier masters plow in straight run, he is ready for snowplow turn, carried out by pulling back uphill shoulder, shifting weight onto uphill ski, keeping outer side of body (*above*) in comma through fall line. After he masters snowplow, skier can try stem turn, in which tail of uphill ski only is thrust out while downhill ski briefly holds original direction.

Final fruition of shortswing is parallel turn made by heel thrust alone after tails of skis have been unweighted with lift from pole. To get from stem turn to parallel swing through fall line, skier should practice stem-turn-swing where he gets feel of controlled heel thrust on long swing into slope after turn toward the fall line. Next he modifies stem with heel-brushing stem swing, then eliminates stem by using pole to start parallel swing.

83